Giving God the Worst of Me

Dana K. White

Copyright © 2015 Dana K. White

All rights reserved. No portion of this book may be used or reproduced without written permission from the author.

Editing by Mary Carver

Cover design by Jeff Stapleton

Discounts for bulk sales are available. Please contact the author at aslobcomesclean@gmail.com.

ISBN-13: 978-1511466097

DEDICATION

To God: You've taken me on a journey I would never have chosen, but it's so much better than the one I had in mind.

To my family: Your infinite patience and support continually amaze me.

To my readers: Thanks for laughing at my jokes.

CONTENTS

1	My Life According to Plan	1
2	The God Part of All This	3
3	My Version of Control	10
4	Becoming a Mom and Realizing Control is a Delusion	12
5	Maybe I Wasn't Perfect	17
6	A Lifetime of Messiness	21
7	Accepting Responsibility Isn't the End of the Story	26
8	Life Went on in the Messy House	29
9	Trudging On With All My Crazy Ideas	31
10	The Burning Fire of Creativity	34
11	From One Obsession to the Next	36
12	Meanwhile, Spiritual Growth Was Happening	41
13	The Day God Spoke	45
14	Where Do I Start?	49
15	My First Comment	51
16	Me Working On My House. God Working in Me	53
17	Blogging Gets More Serious and I Show My Face	55
18	The Blog's Second Year	58
19	On the Blog	63
20	My Next Big Blogging Mindset Change	66

| 21 | Still So Far From Perfect | 70 |
| 22 | Five Years In | 77 |

MY LIFE ACCORDING TO PLAN

I have a deep, dark secret.

I'll tell it to you soon, but first I'll tell you about me. And why my secret felt so deep and so dark.

As a child, I delivered fantastic speeches . . . in the bathtub. I don't remember if I was accepting awards or speaking to large crowds gathered in stadiums, but I do know the imaginary people were listening. They were sitting on the edges of their seats, holding their breath so they didn't miss a word.

I spoke on a number of riveting topics, but one of my favorite, show-stopping, stun-them-all statements was . . . "I will NEVER say I had a happy childhood."

I lied.

I had a blissful childhood.

I thought I was deprived because I didn't have a Barbie Dream House and my Baptist parents wouldn't let me take dance classes. But really . . . life was good.

Imagination was encouraged and my parents were involved. I never truly doubted I was loved. I felt full support as I grew and tackled various things. And I did lots of things. Lots of different things.

Lots of different, fun, exciting things.

But the main thing I wanted to do? Be a mom.

I wasn't in a *hurry* to be one, but it was my end goal. I carefully planned out my life, determined to fulfill my various dreams at *just* the right times in my life schedule so I'd be ready to throw myself into being a mom when that time came, with no regrets.

I planned out my life and lived it according to plan. Makes me sound super-duper organized, right?

Right.

This was how I viewed life.

Like I was the one in control.

THE GOD PART OF ALL THIS

I'm a Christian. That identity worked well with my life-planning-obsession. It made sense to me that if I did all the right things, God's plan would be whatever my plan was.

As a kid giving speeches in the bathtub, I was terribly sad that I didn't have a more exciting story to tell. A more dramatic testimony of the moment when I realized my need for Jesus/God.

I was young when I became a Christian.

Very young.

Too young to have done drugs or been to prison. I'd never had a single life-threatening illness, nor had I been lost in the woods for days on end.

Phooey.

I LOVED hearing exciting testimonies in church. I loved the stories of dramatic changes that could only happen when a person surrendered her life to a God who loved her and had a plan for her.

I resented my own boring story.

I sought excitement *within* my testimony. My very favorite Sundays were the ones when missionaries came to our church. They showed slides of foreign lands and told stories of the people they met. I literally got chills (I still do) every time someone would tell of helping another person find their way to Christ. (Christ = Jesus = God)

When I was around seven, a missionary couple with a particularly dramatic life spoke to the children at our church. I don't remember where they were working at the time, but I do remember the wife telling about her childhood, several years of which were spent in a concentration camp. I was fascinated. I could picture her living quarters and I cried when she talked of eating food with maggots in it.

That evening, I called my mother into my bedroom and closed the door. "Mom" (I paused for effect), "I believe God is calling me to be a missionary when I grow up."

And I grew up, always having "be a missionary" as my goal.

"Be a mom" fit well with that, so there wasn't any conflict between my two dreams. And I was always coming up with ways to work my other passions into these dreams.

As I became obsessed with theatre, I dreamed of how I could use those skills in missions.

In college, I worked toward becoming a teacher because that was a profession I knew could be useful in missions. I took the only Teaching English as a Second Language class my university offered. When my Dad had a business trip scheduled to Hong Kong, he took my mother and me along so I could see that part of the world. (See how supportive they were of my dreams?)

At the end of college, it was time to make things happen. A woman in my church had a niece who taught overseas with a Christian organization. She told me many times that I should look into it. I agreed I should. But I didn't. I was overwhelmed with student teaching and moving home. I was also actively applying to and auditioning for MFA programs. (MFA = Master of Fine Arts.)

Then one day, an application packet arrived at my college apartment. The woman in my church had given her niece my address, and someone sent me the application. It was thick and detailed, but it was in my hands. The future I wanted had arrived at my doorstep.

I filled it out and mailed it.

After I graduated in December, I worked as a substitute teacher while attempting to figure out what I was going to do next. In February, someone called regarding the application I'd mailed the previous fall. School administrators from all over the world were at the organization's headquarters hiring for the next year. A woman asked me a few questions and said she was putting me through to a principal from Indonesia. The school was in the mountains and the average temperature year round was 70 degrees.

Sure. Sounds good. I like 70 degrees.

I started talking to a man. He asked me questions and then described their location. When he mentioned the heat, I was a little confused, but didn't think much of it.

In our second conversation a few weeks later, we somehow cleared up the misunderstanding about which Southeast Asian country we were discussing. He was in Bangkok, Thailand, where it is most definitely NOT 70 degrees year round.

Or almost ever.

I said I would go. Move to Thailand.

It was a big decision, but it made sense to me. I'd always wanted to be a missionary. I'd always wanted to live in another country. I wanted to teach Theatre. The opportunity to do all these things at once basically fell into my lap at a time when I had absolutely no reason NOT to go.

My attempts to get a paid assistantship for graduate school had failed. I was young and single and had nothing holding me to a specific place. While I was consciously deciding I'd be okay being single forever, I also felt if I ever **did** get married, I'd be glad I'd already fulfilled this dream.

Yep. This was the time.

And then the next week, an old "friend" called. He asked if I wanted to go to a movie with some other people. **I had no earthly idea if this was a date or not**, but I went. After much awkward signal-reading, he paid.

We'd been a part of a group of friends who spent time together in the summers during college. Almost everyone else in the group had already married and moved away. We were the only two left, so I didn't know if we were hanging out as friends or if something else was afoot.

But I knew I liked him.

Liked-him liked-him.

So when he called the next week to ask me to go on another maybe-a-date-maybe-not, I was frustrated to have to tell him I couldn't go. I had a commitment I couldn't cancel.

I did my best to explain I'd love to do anything else at any other time, but it didn't work. He felt shot down and didn't call the next weekend.

In the next few weeks (while he wasn't calling), I took the big step of signing the teaching contract, agreeing (in writing) to move half-way across the world and live in another country (*half-way across the* **world**) for two whole years.

Right *after* I signed that contract, he called again.

It was on our second date-or-not-who-knows that I *knew*. I knew he was **the one**.

How? As we were driving home, things got silly. He pulled out the black case for his glasses and said he sometimes pretended it was a cell phone so people in other cars would think he had one.

(It was the 90s. Not everyone had a cell phone.)

I took that and ran with it. I don't remember what all I said into that pretend phone, but I'm sure it was hilarious. He . . . was even more hilarious. We laughed and laughed and laughed.

I came home and immediately called a friend to tell her I was going to marry him.

"He . . . gets me," I explained. "You know that part of my sense of humor that not everyone gets? He gets it."

But that wasn't all. I *knew* this guy. I'd known him for years as a friend. Even before that, I knew OF him from mutual close friends. We had nothing to hide.

Once the "spark" combined with what I already knew about his character, I fell hard.

And so began six months of maybe-we're-dating/I-really-really-hope-we're-dating that finally ended in a DTR (Define The Relationship talk) just before I moved to Thailand. *Two weeks* before.

It was a whirlwind that made me feel tumbly-bumbly in a very good way, *and* it fit perfectly into my overall plan.

I could see God's hand. I could see His timing.

Each of those first phone calls came immediately AFTER I'd taken another step of commitment to moving to Thailand. By the time we admitted what was happening and became "official" I had a non-refundable plane ticket. I was happy I didn't have to choose between the love of my life and my dreams of living overseas. It looked like I was going to be able to do both.

Not that it was angst-less. About six weeks before I left for Thailand (while things were still unspoken/uncertain between us), I took a group of teenagers to the camp where I'd worked as a short-term missionary for several summers in high school and college. I LOVED this camp. So much of my spiritual growth happened there, and I was excited to go back.

Life was crazy. I was falling in love and preparing to move to the other side of the world. I longed for the peace and focus this place had always provided.

But when I got there, I sat on my favorite lakeside bench . . . and nothing happened. I tried to pray. I tried to read my Bible.

Zilch. Nada.

It was as if there was a huge wall between God and me and I couldn't figure out how to tear it down. This went on for the entire week. I was angry that I couldn't re-create the feelings and experiences and closeness to God I'd felt every other time I was there.

On the last night of camp, we started singing my favorite song. It is a very old song I've never heard ANYwhere else. The chorus goes like this:

> Lord, send me anywhere. Only go with me. Lay any burden on me, only sustain me.

And then came the part that cut into my heart. The part I *couldn't* make myself sing:

> Sever any tie, save the tie that binds me to your heart.

Ummmm, what??

That was it. That was the problem.

I was excited about moving to Thailand. I was ready to be the missionary I'd dreamed of being since I was a little girl. I loved the drama and the idea of stepping out on faith.

But I was holding something back. If I was truly giving all of myself to God, if I was really going to let Him do whatever He wanted to do with me in Thailand, I had to be willing for Him to sever any tie. ANY tie. Even the one with that cute-and-hairy guy I "knew" I would marry.

I needed to accept that serving God meant I wasn't the one in control of how my life turned out. If I stayed, I could wiggle my way into this guy's life plans. I could be proactive and intentional and make things happen. Good things.

But saying good-bye, even knowing I was doing what God had clearly set up for me to do, meant there was absolutely no guarantee I would marry the man of my dreams. In fact, I was putting myself into a position that kills many relationships.

Amidst tears and blubbering (that surely scared every kid on the trip), I said, "OK."

"OK. I'll go. Even if it means I ultimately lose this thing I want and that I *really believe* is a gift from You."

The wall was gone. The thing stopping me from praying, from gaining insight and understanding when I read the Bible? It was gone.

Just because I said, "OK."

I let go of the control of my own life.

I didn't want to, but I was *willing* to give up this great guy if God's plan for my life didn't include him.

Thankfully, though, I didn't have to give him up. The moment I arrived home from camp, our relationship took off and I never again questioned what was going on between us.

Whew.

God's timing? It was working, and I was totally on board with it.

I'd live in Thailand while the man of my dreams finished grad school. Logic and planning told me this was a great combination. I could do the thing I had always wanted to do. He could focus on getting his Master's degree without the distraction of me!

And that's pretty much how it worked. After two years of daily emails and several in-person visits, we got married twenty days after I moved back to Texas from Thailand.

God's plans jiving perfectly with my own plans seemed logical and right to me.

MY VERSION OF CONTROL

I don't want to pretend I did everything perfectly. I didn't. I made plenty of mistakes and was a master procrastinator.

But I was also a master of tunnel vision. Tunnel vision was my personal secret weapon.

I *loved* being in the Tunnel Vision Zone. Give me a big project and I'm in my element. Put me in charge of a huge event and I'm happy.

I'd look at my calendar and know that for six weeks here or four days there, I would be completely zoned in on a certain big task.

I would focus on every detail and produce a finished product that made me proud.

I think this is why I love theatre so much. I was born with a flair for the dramatic and I can work up tears on command, but really, I love the *control*.

Life on stage is life under control.

I clearly remember the first time I was asked to direct a series of scenes within a play. I was a junior in college.

Something happened in the depths of my soul when I started telling people where to stand and exactly when to fall off the couch.

I was in *control*. I was the one who determined how this particular snippet of life happened. I shaped it in a way that made people laugh or cry or gasp at precisely the right moment.

It tickled my Control Bone like nothing ever had. And I loved it.

When I taught theatre (first overseas and then as a newlywed), I continued what had become my way of life. I would spend a month or so living "normally," cooking dinner each night and getting to bed before 10. Then, I'd throw everything normal to the side for two months while I obsessed over a production. I skipped meal planning and shoved fast food into my mouth between painting sets and shopping for costumes and designing programs.

(Thankfully, the husband was pretty easy-going and went along for the ride.)

Basically, **I was good at obsessing**. I was in my element when I could tackle something huge, make it great, and then sit back and enjoy the results. The only (small, fairly irrelevant) side effect was that I let *everything* else go. I put anything non-big-project-related on hold until the project was finished. And then I played catch up.

And then I started another huge project.

And put everything else on hold.

And caught up when it was over.

It seemed like a logical way to live.

BECOMING A MOM AND REALIZING CONTROL IS A DELUSION

And then . . . I had a baby.

Baby-making had gone mostly according to plan and I was in my element during pregnancy. Like other times I'd stepped into the unknown, I prepared. I read books. I went to classes.

I developed my game plan.

I watched *A Baby Story* on TLC *every single day* in the months before my first child was born. I decided I was going to be the woman who was strong and courageous and handled the pain like a pro. I *liked* her.

I didn't like the laboring mother who whined. Who cried and whimpered at the pain. I had zero patience for the woman whose husband looked embarrassed because people in the hall were scared by his wife's moans and screams.

And then I went into labor.

I had just spent Christmas in my own home, resting on the couch as my mother and sister-in-law cooked in my kitchen. The baby was due on January 6th. On December 27th, Hubby and I went to a doctor's appointment where we were told our baby wasn't coming any time soon.

We planned to go to the mall to exchange a Christmas gift, but I was suddenly tired.

Crazy tired.

I couldn't go one . . . more . . . *step* and I just wanted to go home. We'd return the shirt the next day.

Except the next day, I went into labor. I was embarrassed to call the doctor since he'd been adamant I had a week or so left to be pregnant. I was NOT going to be one of those crazy people who were turned away from the hospital for having "imaginary" contractions.

(I know they're not imaginary. I just said it that way to emphasize my confidence that I was going to do this motherhood thing well. *Right from the get go.*)

Finally, after moaning and groaning and yelling at the top of my lungs for hours, I made my husband call the doctor at three in the afternoon. As expected, he didn't believe us. But since I had been writing down the exact times and lengths of my contractions, he couldn't argue with my carefully recorded data.

We drove 25 minutes to the hospital and I started asking about an epidural as soon as we parked. Those women on TV who kept it all under control? *They must have been robots.*

I was the woman I hated. I cried, whined, and generally lamented until that lovely needle went into my spine.

I wasn't even upset when the doctor decided to do an emergency c-section. Perfect birth? Whatever. Let's just get this over with.

See how incredibly practical I am?

My son was born and I fell in love immediately. (I was prepared to *not* fall in love, though, since I'd read all those books about every possible scenario for brand new motherhood.)

We took him home three days later, and my universe began to tilt. My desire for control (and my total, unwavering belief that it was possible) was strongly challenged.

This little bitty creature hadn't read the books I'd read. He didn't seem to understand I was more than willing to take on any challenges *as long as they had been covered in the text.*

The main issue was that my baby had a mind of his own. He decided right after we got home from the hospital that our feeding arrangement wasn't working for him. No amount of coaxing could make him see things my way. Every three hours (I'd read the books, remember?), I would tell him it was time to eat and he would tell me (loudly) he didn't agree. I was shocked at his strength (and ear-piercing volume) as I used every ounce of my own strength to convince him to do things my way.

In case you're confused, I'm talking about breastfeeding. I had been to the *class*, and I'd read the *books*. I knew about the football hold and foremilk and such. I *didn't* know that some babies can't latch on. I definitely didn't know that some babies don't even WANT to breastfeed when it's difficult.

For six solid weeks, each feeding session was deafening. He screamed bloody murder and resisted with every (amazingly strong) fiber of his eight-pound-being. I put on the calm and firm mommy voice I had practiced on my dolls for years, and explained he was **going to eat**.

And then I pumped. And he happily took his bottle. And I cried.

Sobbed.

And three hours later (three hours after we started, only an hour after we finished), we tried again.

Those were difficult days. My world was rocked. I couldn't believe this craziness was happening to me. Why? Why was it that after millennia of mothers effortlessly breastfeeding, I was the *only* woman who *ever* had a baby who couldn't latch on to eat. Who didn't WANT to snuggle up to his mom and let her cover herself with a blanket while she sipped icewater and carried on a nice conversation.

And I asked these questions. *Out loud.*

I struggle with Excessive Honesty, so when people asked how things were going, I was incapable of pretending everything was hunky dory.

I was shocked to learn that almost everyone I knew had struggled to breastfeed in the beginning. *Many* babies had to learn how to latch on correctly. Moms everywhere had rented hospital-grade pumps and called lactation consultants and cried themselves to sleep.

But they never talked about it.

Part of me was relieved as I heard story after story of moms and babies who had survived those first few months. Some babies eventually figured it out. Some moms accepted that sixth graders who once drank formula don't look much different from those who weren't weaned until after they could walk.

Not everyone was helpful, but most people were.

The other part of me, though, was mad. I had read the books for cryin' out loud! I had listened to TAPES! I made my husband listen to those tapes and sit through breastfeeding class *with* me!

And yet no one mentioned how hard it could be. No author and no friend. How cracked nipples and clogged milk ducts might be the least of your worries.

As I dug in my heels and eventually won the breastfeeding battle, I saw the beauty of our six weeks of struggle. I had endured. My baby boy finally learned to eat, and he turned into a champion breastfeeder who was a nightmare to wean at thirteen months.

And I had a more realistic view of parenting. I no longer lived under the delusion that things would happen just because I wanted them to happen. I realized this human whose mother I was had his own brain, his own personality, his own quirks and preferences. And parenting wasn't a dictatorship.

Or a business. Or even a classroom.

It was parenting. A unique thing/job/life-calling that was going to suck every emotion and every ounce of energy from my soul.

I also no longer assumed that others were being perfectly honest when they said everything was fine.

And I began to dream of honesty.

This was the time in my life when I developed a passion for helping other moms. For being the one who was willing to admit things weren't always easy. For sharing my learned-the-hard-way wisdom so someone else could get there faster and be spared the misery.

MAYBE I WASN'T PERFECT

Let me explain that even though I had moments of misery, I wasn't miserable. I was exactly where I wanted to be. I was living my dream.

I was a *mom*.

I threw myself into this new identity. It was here. My life's dream had turned into my real life.

But the day in and day out did surprise me.

Mostly, I was shocked to learn other people had known what they were talking about. You *did* do more laundry. Pre-kids, that didn't make sense to me because baby clothes are so **small**. Why would they require their own load? I'll just add them in with ours.

Duh.

But it's not *just* about baby clothes. It's about how Mom never gets to re-wear anything.

Ever.

I was washing my own clothes after each and every wear because they were always covered in milk.

Or puke.

Or snot.

Or worse. *Yes. There's worse.*

And sometimes "worse" happened more than once a day.

One baby can create his own load of laundry in a few hours.

Yes. People were right about laundry.

They were also right about showers and cooking and such. I honestly believed (I'm embarrassed to say this now) that I would be able to teach my baby to play quietly on a blanket (duh, a blanket would be a *boun-da-ry*) while I showered.

I'm not sure what age this fictional child was.

Technically, I could have done this while my son was not yet mobile.

Technically. But I guess I realized on day 1.3 that it wasn't worth trying. Showers aren't relaxing when someone is screaming at the top of his lungs. It's not just the noise, but the guilt. He was happy until I turned on the water. Obviously, I chose hygiene over him and he will never forgive me.

Ever.

But even as I realized I was wrong about oh-so-many things, I determined to grow and learn and be the best mother I could be. My days were full of failures, but I felt that overall, this motherhood gig was exactly what I wanted it to be. I had no interest in delusions, I just wanted to live it fully.

There was just one problem.

(Fine. There were plenty of small problems, but just one big one that boggled my mind. One that felt forever unsolvable.)

It hit me when that baby I loved was four months old.

I was changing his diaper in his room. We were singing or playing or something. (Four months is such a fun, smiley age.)

And then I looked around. I mean, REALLY looked around.

His room . . . was a *wreck*.

Teeny-tiny clothes all over the floor.

Board books spread out around the bookshelf. On the floor. The ones still on the shelf had been haphazardly shoved there.

Toys (and we had . . . like . . . *three*) were strewn across the carpet.

It hit me. Here was this little person who had his own space designated in our home. It was his home too. His space was a disaster area, *but it wasn't his fault*. He was four months old. He couldn't even crawl.

Now let me explain that I wasn't shocked to see a messy room. I didn't have virgin eyes that had never been exposed to clutter or a home in disarray.

I had seen it before. Everywhere I looked and in every space I'd ever called my own.

It's just that it hit me. By "it" I mean reality. **And responsibility.**

My son was four months old, and his room was a wreck. But it was *my* fault that his room was a wreck. I couldn't shift the blame to anyone or anything but me.

And here's where I tell you my deep dark secret:

I am a slob.

A bona-fide, legit, let's-just-be-honest-here slob.

You probably knew that if you knew anything about me before you started reading this book, but I'm talking about a defining moment in my life. **The moment when I realized there was something wrong with me.**

I mentioned earlier that I suffer from Excessive Honesty. I do. But at the same time, I am a master of self-delusion. It's not that I didn't know I was messy before that diaper-changing moment. I knew, *but I had never worried about it*.

I assumed that like so many other things in my life, once I got around to making housekeeping a priority, I'd conquer it.

It wasn't that I didn't *like* a clean house. It wasn't that I was anti-organizing. I LOVED the idea of organizing. I loved flipping through organizing magazines, watching organizing shows and strolling down the organizing aisle.

I had every intention of being organized.

Next. In my next stage of life. In my next job. In my next home.

A LIFETIME OF MESSINESS

I had been messy all my life. The first true memory I have of my intense disorganization was in first grade.

I was a good student. I liked filling in the blanks on worksheets and learning to color inside the lines. I was one of the first to get my ENTIRE behavior card stamped with itty-bitty smiley faces.

But then, one day, my mother sent me to school with a trash bag.

I was confused.

The night before, we'd had an open house. Parents came into the classroom to ooh and aah over art projects and see how their precious first grader spent his/her days.

My mother stumbled upon my cubby.

Now, a *cubby* is a delicious thought. In my mind, it produces visions of carefully chosen treasures and neatly stacked school supplies.

Mine wasn't like that. It wouldn't even close because of the sixty or seventy (or three hundred) too many papers I'd shoved in it.

It was a mess.

A big, paper-ey mess. And my mother was horrified. And embarrassed. She explained that I was to put everything from my cubby into the bag and bring it home. We would go through the papers together and see what we needed to keep.

Huh. Mmm-kay.

Then there was the time my fourth grade teacher called me out to the hall on a Monday morning. She looked distressed and confused. *I was her teacher's pet.* She knew she could call on me to help other kids or when she needed to know someone was actually listening.

Apparently . . . she had been in the room on Sunday when an incident occurred. This was a small Christian school and the attached church used our classrooms for Sunday School. Somehow . . . my desk was overturned.

Out poured seventy-thousand (ish) dirty tissues.

I could make the excuse that it was likely allergy season. *But still . . .*

My teacher was shocked. Horrified. Perplexed.

I was embarrassed.

Any small space I could call my own turned into a Disaster Zone, but even though I was perpetually disorganized, **it never occurred to me** that the next phase of my life wouldn't be completely different. I *liked* organized spaces, and I could picture them in my head. I could plan them. I never doubted my intelligence, so I never doubted my ability to one day get things under control.

One day. Y'know, *when it actually mattered.*

At first, I thought One Day would come in Junior High. I had a locker, and some entrepreneur somewhere had already figured out (back in the 80s) that there was a virtual goldmine in the locker accessories business. Shelves. Mirrors. All sorts of things to keep a locker neat and organized. So I bought them (all) and carefully installed my pretty red shelves. My locker looked fantastic . . . right up until school started. As soon as papers and books and such were added to the mix, the shelves became a way to separate the stacks. The messy stacks.

The stacks that burst out of the locker every time I opened the door.

I have oh-so-many examples. Basically, they all involve me setting up a room or space perfectly. I'd designate areas for various things to happen. "This is where I'll put dirty laundry!" "Shoes will go in this nifty shoe-thingy that has a picture of a beautifully organized closet on the package!"

Then I would start using the space. Living in it.

And all would go to chaos. Dirty laundry didn't end up in its perfect little spot. *It covered the entire floor.* The shoe-organizer hung whompy-jawed (and empty) in the closet while shoes were scattered wherever I absent-mindedly kicked them off my feet.

To me, cleaning meant putting laundry in the dirty laundry spot and shoes in the shoe-organizer. THEN I could worry about dusting and vacuuming and such. But it was always such a HUGE job (to declutter first so I could clean) that I'd find wonderful reasons to put it off again and again.

Every living space I had became a disaster area, but I functioned. Sure, I spent more time than I wanted to looking for that other shoe, but my grades were great, I was involved in everything from school plays to student government, and when people needed an event organized, I was the go to girl.

I didn't love the messy space, but I didn't *worry* about it. It wasn't my focus at that time in my life. I had better things to do. Someday, when it *was* my focus, I'd get everything spiffed up.

I kept my faith in this delusion all through college and into my single years. Through my messy dorm rooms and messy apartments.

I'm pretty sure I even reassured my soon-to-be-husband after his jaw dropped when he saw my bedroom for the very first time. The floor was covered in stuff. I probably had some good excuse about being busy planning a wedding or whatever.

I had lots of those. Excuses, I mean.

But I didn't view them as excuses. They were **reasons**. As a hyper-logical person, I saw nothing lame about them.

Then I got married.

I assumed getting married would solve my messiness problem.

Why? For the first time ever, it would *matter*.

My home would be part of my identity. In every other phase of my life, my identity was outside my home. It was in my classroom or on a stage or in the work that I did.

But now I was a wife.

When I registered for wedding gifts, I was living in this dream world. I was in a time crunch since I was only home (in the U.S.) for a few weeks over Christmas break. I saw cups and plates and platters and pictured lovely dinners with friends in an uncluttered dining room.

So I registered for them. All of them. At least four sets.

And we got *all* of those dishes. **All of them.**

When we married, my husband was 32 and I was 25. Most of our friends were already married and people were excited for us. We'd had time to establish ourselves as adults, so we were given gifts from childhood friends, college friends, church friends and work friends.

It was amazing how many gifts we received.

But at the same time, we were combining the stuff we already had. The stuff he'd had as a bachelor living on his own and the stuff I stored from my college apartment while I lived in Thailand.

We rented a "One Bedroom with Den" apartment SIMPLY SO WE COULD STORE MY STUFF. Right. The den (which would have been called a bedroom except you had to walk through it to get to the only bathroom . . .) was stacked to the ceiling with stuff. Boxes.

Boxes I hadn't opened since I graduated from college two and a half years earlier.

Oh. And there were boxes lining the walls of the dining area as well. We basically lived in a storage unit. But I believed with all my heart that we needed that stuff for someday.

Someday I would be Dana Homemaker. I would rock the housekeeping thing.

After all, being an awesome homemaker was part of my *plan*.

It did seem strange that I hadn't been magically cured of my disorganization issues because I got married and actually WANTED to be organized. But . . . I was teaching. Full time. And I was a *theatre* teacher, so I was directing rehearsals after school.

Who in their right mind would expect someone to do all that AND keep a house neat and tidy? Crazy people. That's who.

I was disappointed my assumption that I'd be cured once I got married was wrong, but I didn't worry too much. Once I had kids? *Then* I'd be organized.

Obviously.

I was going to be a stay at home mom. What else would I have to do?

ACCEPTING RESPONSIBILITY ISN'T THE END OF THE STORY

Standing there in that nursery with my four month old baby, I realized I was the problem. I'd been blaming circumstances and people and life stages all my life.

It was a slap in the face. For someone who was prideful about intentional living and not wasting a moment and being a purposeful mom, I didn't relish admitting something was wrong.

But I finally accepted nothing magical was ever going to happen to make me organized.

My perfectly planned picture wasn't matching up with my reality. Yes, I was reading to my baby, but I had to shove clutter to the other end of the couch so we'd have a place to snuggle.

Admitting I had a problem might have been the first step, but it didn't actually solve anything. I did seek to be purposeful. I started reading books and websites and asking around to learn how others kept their homes under control. But the cycle continued.

I lived my life the way I always had.

In project mode.

I would resolve to change. I'd clean and clean all day every day for a week. But somehow, my house didn't look much better.

I would schedule a party. THAT would get me cleaning! And it did. I set aside two weeks. First, I would declutter (which really just meant throwing everything in the master bedroom and locking the door) and then I would clean. (Because you can't actually clean when there's clutter everywhere.)

I would look around my clean house and sigh with contentment. THIS was what I wanted my house to look like! I just needed to keep it this way. Maintain! That's the key, right? Get it perfect and then keep it perfect!

Three days later I would look up and gasp. My house was back to being as bad as it was before I even started cleaning for the party.

I had no idea what had happened in those three days.

And that was my main frustration. Not knowing. Not being able to figure this thing out, even though it WAS my focus. Even though it WAS the time in my life when I was ready for it to happen.

I kept trying and kept failing.

With each failure, I became more discouraged. The only thing I learned was that another method didn't work for me.

I added two more babies and keeping the house under control became harder and harder. Harder to do something I couldn't do anyway.

I saw a promo for a certain expert-on-everything-based talk-show. The next day's show was going to tell the story of a hopelessly messy woman whom they had helped! They had fixed her home and the host's words of advice were going to change this woman's life forever!

I was determined to watch that episode. Practical advice for the chronically disorganized? Sign me up! I liked this guy's no-nonsense advice on other topics so maybe he was going to say something that would rock my world and cure me for good!

The people from the show went into the woman's house, installed shelves and cubbies and such, and cleaned it up for her. She came to the studio for her earth-shattering consultation and was told, "We're going to show up unannounced one day, so you're going to keep it that way, right?"

And that was basically it.

Maybe he said some other things, but not much. I was so discouraged, and **I realized mine wasn't a legit problem.** If psychologists and professional organizers didn't see a reason to dig a little deeper and consider that maybe there was more of an issue here than someone not being afraid enough of an impending doorbell, then there was something truly wrong with me.

I even started a letter to that talk show. (I never actually sent it . . .) I wanted to beg for real help. To explain that I truly believed there was something wrong with me. Something mentally wrong. Something in my brain that just didn't get it.

Someone else sticking things into organizing bins for me wouldn't help. I knew this. My dear mother had tried that over and over, even after I was married. I basically had an on-call professional organizer at my service.

Yes. It looked *fabulous* when she finished.

Yes. I swore *every single time* that I would keep it going.

But eventually I stopped swearing. I knew my resolutions were a lie. This had absolutely nothing to do with me wanting it. **I did want it.** I was desperate to change, but the struggle was so incredibly difficult.

The eyes of the woman on that talk show haunted me. I believed I saw through them, into her soul. When the host told her his earth-shattering, life-changing advice was that she should be ready for a surprise visit . . . she smiled and nodded. When he asked if she was going to keep it up (out of gratefulness that he had sent someone in to solve her problem), she nodded. Hesitantly.

She knew. She knew it wasn't going to happen.

And I was convinced that no one (except that poor woman) was ever going to understand. And no one was *ever* going to be able to help me.

LIFE WENT ON IN THE MESSY HOUSE

"And no one was ever going to be able to help me . . . "

Wow. That was a downer.

But really, it's not like I cried my way through the days as I sat in piles of clutter. No. I LIVED in the midst of that clutter. I kept on doing my best. In fits and spurts I would do better at keeping up with the house, but it would always slip back into disaster.

Meanwhile, I loved my Mom Job. I planned birthday parties with creative, homemade cakes. I cooked almost every night. (From scratch!) I shoved piles of mail to one end of the kitchen table so we could decorate Christmas cookies on the other end.

I organized groups for stay-at-home moms and sang in the church choir. I wrote and directed large-scale Christmas productions. I functioned. My kids were fed and bathed and almost always had clean clothes to wear.

But I couldn't do everything I wanted to do. I couldn't fully be the mom I'd always wanted to be.

I couldn't have anyone over without plenty of notice and LOTS of work. I'd always imagined I would be the mother who welcomed friends into her home at a moment's notice. Need a place for a playdate? Come on over! Let's drink coffee and talk while the kids run around!

And that was my frustration. In previous life phases, my life was outside my home. But now, my home was where life happened. My identity and my environment were all wrapped up together.

Ugh.

TRUDGING ON WITH ALL MY CRAZY IDEAS

Having "arrived" at being a mother didn't mean I stopped my dreaming and planning. I was always coming up with ideas of businesses or ministries I could start one day.

Then I made a new friend who was a fanatical eBay seller. She kept telling me I needed to try it.

eBay. *Hmmmmmmm.*

Most of my big ideas were for the future. They were for when my kids would be a little older.

But eBay was something I could do from my house. Right then.

(Slightly higher-pitched.) Hmmmmmmm.

It started with sheer frustration over all the junk in my home.

I had a lot of stuff.

Remember those six sets of dishes? And the room full of stuff we didn't need in our first apartment?

Right.

When we moved into our first home, I had no more excuses. There was no more "waiting for someday." With three bedrooms, a real-life living room, and a two car garage, I knew logic didn't allow for us to have huge amounts of items in storage anymore.

So one January, I started purging stuff. My eBay expert friend encouraged and instructed me as I began creating online auctions.

I started with some new-in-the-box wedding gifts we hadn't used in four years.

These were the *obvious* things to sell. If we hadn't used them yet, we probably never would. They needed to go. I made some decent money on those first sales and was thrilled. $47 is a lot of money to a mama who hasn't had any way whatsoever to scrape up extra money in a few years.

I sold a juicer, an iced-tea maker, a milkshake maker and more.

It was exciting.

And then one day, I spotted a little something at a garage sale.

I LOVED garage sales. *Loved 'em.*

I loved them so much that I'd get myself and my babies out of bed before 7 a.m. to go "garage sale-ing" with a friend who loved them too. *Every single week.*

I remember the exact sale where I saw that little green box. It was "vintage" and even though I had no idea what it was, *I knew it was cool.*

I picked it up and found a metal, old-fashioned rhinestone applicator. A little machine for sparkling up t-shirts or denim or whatever you wanted to make fancy.

But the kicker was . . . it was only ten cents.

Ten measly cents.

How in the world could a bargain-loving, eBay aspiring girl like me NOT take it home?

So I did. And I sold it for a whopping $17.43.

I was hooked. Buying for pennies and selling for dollars was exciting. I now know I have always had an entrepreneurial spirit. At the time I just knew I was in love with eBay.

I started buying more and more stuff at garage sales, hoping I could sell it online. I was learning as I went. Unfortunately, I was buying faster than I was learning. I would buy wall-hangings and baby toys and bookends, and THEN learn that half of them were worthless. I also learned there are ideal times to sell seasonal items, so I would buy things and wait.

And the things that were worthless mixed in with the things that needed to wait. Together they began filling up my house.

My already too-full house.

But eBay was a *project*. A project that was making me, a full-time stay-at-home mom, some nice little chump change. We could grab fast food at the end of the month when our eating-out envelope was empty. I could buy some new (on clearance) jeans when I needed them.

Like my big theatre productions, eBay was another area where I was super-duper organized. While dishes piled up in the sink and dust escaped my notice, I was proud of my system. It might be a regular thing to search desperately for clean undies for the family, but I could wash, dry and photograph a load of kids' clothes I'd bought at garage sales with laser focus.

I had shipping labels and packing materials and a postal scale that were always put back in their designated homes. I could find what I needed when I needed it. THOSE things had a place. They were a project. And projects were things I could control.

It was the other stuff (ALL the other stuff) that boggled my mind.

THE BURNING FIRE OF CREATIVITY

Creativity burns in my soul and it has to find a place to vent to keep me from exploding.

Theatre is my art form of choice, but the hours involved didn't fit well with being a mom of little ones.

When I got a new camera, my brain churned with ideas of how to turn *that* into a business. *I just couldn't figure out how to make it something that wouldn't take me away from my family in the evenings or on weekends.*

I once bought a whole slew of frames at a garage sale and imagined myself painting them in funky colors and turning *that* into a business. (Unfortunately, my creativity *doesn't* come with an eye for color.)

All my Quest for a Creative Outlet ideas kept coming back to writing. Writing plays, writing books, writing for magazines. When writing-related brainstorms passed through, they made the most sense.

Writing was a thing I could do and not leave my home.

It was something I was good at. (So good I even know that sentence should actually be "It was something at which I was good.")

But I didn't write without a reason. I wasn't a journaler. Without knowing someone was actually going to read what I wrote, I had no desire to just write for the sake of writing.

(Hmmm. Kind of like I didn't see the point of cleaning if no one was coming over . . .)

But every time I had a *reason* to write, I received much-coveted affirmation.

When my oldest was an infant, I was in charge of recruiting discussion leaders for our church's moms' group. I wrote a letter. A letter that clearly explained what was needed and properly tugged at the hearts of the women who were being asked.

I enjoyed writing the letter, but didn't think much of it until several people approached me to tell me how beautiful the letter was. Their focus was on the quality of writing. They didn't actually volunteer to be discussion leaders, but they were impressed with my writing.

And I thought, hmmmmm.

Soon after that, I was asked to direct our church's Christmas production. This wasn't just a concert with a few choral numbers. It was a full-scale show with 300+ people. At the first meeting (in April), it became clear as we brainstormed that the music minister was planning for me to write the script.

Ummm, *what?*

Yes. I had dreams of writing, but I didn't have dreams of writing *this*.

But I did it. And I enjoyed it.

The next year, I went into the meetings as someone who was going to write a script. *As a writer.* It was confirmed to me that writing was a gift I had been given by God, and that it was something I could fit into my life of naptimes and days spent at home with my kids.

Still, though, I only dreamed about turning it into a career in a vague, someday-when-I-have-time-to-figure-out-how-to-make-it-happen kind of way.

FROM ONE OBSESSION TO THE NEXT

Through eBay and generally being online more than I ever had before, I discovered the underworld of couponers.

I'd heard about these people, but didn't know there were communities of them online. I thought each one figured it all out for herself. One day I stumbled upon a little online group of Dallas couponers and started lurking. I began to learn their language. They shared tips. They talked about bargains grabbed for pennies on the dollar.

After watching for about a month, I decided to attempt to replicate one of their shopping trips. I followed every little step and walked out of a drugstore with arms full of stuff for just a few dollars. ***And*** I had a piece of paper in my hand that claimed I could walk right back in and use it like money to get even more stuff.

I was hooked.

I began waking up every morning, desperate to find out what new deals had materialized. I lay in bed at night creating perfect coupon scenarios.

It became my new obsession.

eBay fell to the wayside as I realized I was saving as much money each month as I once made selling.

And then, someone in my couponing group linked to a website called MoneySavingMom.com.

What? A website? About coupons? You mean, not a closed group like this one?

I clicked over, and I was fascinated.

I saw this website referred to itself as a blog. It linked to other websites called blogs.

I'd heard of blogs, but had *no idea* what they were. All I knew was that a certain talk-show-host on a certain multi-woman daytime show had one. I'd hear about controversy happening on the show and then I'd hear she went home and "blogged" about it.

And that was what blogs were to me. A place where people ranted and raged about politics and other controversial topics.

But when I ran across MoneySavingMom.com in April of 2008 and realized what blogs actually were, a fire was lit within my soul.

This was *it*.

My dreams of being a writer? With the click of a few buttons, I could achieve them. Like, tomorrow.

I saw women who were writing and reaching real readers in real time. People were reading blogs. And women were turning these blogs into businesses.

Sign. Me. Up.

For real.

Y'know how I mentioned before that I wasn't a journaler? I needed to have a purpose. Writing for the sake of writing didn't make much sense to me, but writing and knowing someone somewhere might actually read it? That *was* for me.

The wheels of my imagination started turning. Bigtime. I researched how to set up a blog, how to build one, and how to make money from one.

But I didn't start one.

I had a name, I had a theme. I was going to call it Allergic to Bonbons. Tagline: So what do you *do* all day?

The idea was that since I'm allergic to chocolate, I couldn't completely fulfill the stereotype of a stay-at-home mom who the world assumes sits on her couch and eats bonbons.

So what *did* I do all day?

That's a common question stay-at-home-moms get, and I was passionate about answering it. I wanted to teach people how to coupon, how to use freezer-cooking strategies to get supper on the table simply and quickly. I wanted to share how I clothed my kids in garage sale bargains and used eBay to earn a little extra spending money each month.

I wanted to write about motherhood. About all the parts of being a mom where I felt I had something of value to share.

Remember all that purposefulness earlier? It had paid off! It was time to share my brilliance with the world. If I could do it, anyone could!

Self-sufficiency? Yay for that!!!

Except one thing. One little old, deep-dark-secret thing.

My house.

I couldn't do it. I couldn't let myself take on yet another project that I knew would consume me. I couldn't let *one more thing* take my focus away from my home.

Remember eBay? Remember coupons? I was still couponing, and like eBay, it was fueling this odd, obsessive-compulsive part of me. I spent hours cutting and filing coupons. I organized my shopping trips to be things of efficient beauty.

If you saw my system, you'd think I had OCD and my house had never seen a dust bunny.

Meanwhile, my dishes remained undone, outgrown clothes lay at the bottom of laundry piles that were never finished, and I lived in constant fear of unexpected doorbells.

I knew my focus would be sucked into blogging, but that wasn't the only thing that kept me from starting. It was fear.

I was passionate about my job as a mother. I wanted to share that passion with a world of moms I knew were bewildered and lonely. I wanted to encourage moms by writing things that were good and true and helpful.

But I was afraid. I feared someone would find out what my house really looked like. That it was a sometimes-knee-deep mess. That I couldn't remember the last time I cleaned toilets or mopped the kitchen floor.

I couldn't handle the thought of being a fraud. I knew that being a mom is generally seen as going hand in hand with keeping house. My inability to do both well was a huge source of shame for me. A shame I tried desperately to keep hidden.

So I waited. I dreamed about that blog, and ached as I saw blog after blog with ideas similar to mine pop up and gain traction.

But I wasn't JUST waiting.

I was cleaning.

While this messiness had been a source of shame and frustration before, I now had a different kind of motivation.

The messiness was keeping me from living my dream. Some bloggers fall into blogging. They start sharing stories with family members and it turns into something else.

That wasn't me. Before I set up a site or wrote a single post, I had plans to create a community and turn it into a business.

I dreamed and I ached and I planned. And I tried to get my house under control.

I would do great for a few days. Sometimes I would even make it a week or two. In a rare case, three!

Then life would happen. My house would go back to being a disaster. And whatever new "system" I was trying would get listed in the Failure Column in my brain.

I'd get confirmation that *there was something truly wrong with me*. Systems that made other people skip around with joy didn't work for me.

No matter what I tried, the lightswitch never flipped in my brain. I always felt I was hanging on by my fingernails, never truly in control because I knew at any moment I would lose my grip.

I kept searching for the magic cure. For the phrase or moment or system that would help it all click in my head and change my messy ways.

But each time the click didn't happen, I became more pessimistic, and more certain there was no hope for me.

MEANWHILE, SPIRITUAL GROWTH WAS HAPPENING

Spiritual growth. Hmmmm. How to explain that bit of Christianese to the random non-church-type reader? Well, let me explain how my own spiritual growth happened in these years and maybe that will help.

As I mentioned before, I grew up in a church-going home with parents who identified themselves as Christians. It wasn't until I was an adult, however, that I realized how fortunate I was to grow up in that specific home. I learned that not all who identify themselves as Christians live the way my parents did/do.

They didn't *just* go to church. They read the Bible (all of it) and sought to apply its advice and principles to every single area of their lives.

This was normal to me.

I didn't know until later that some people only listen while they're sitting in church, retain a little here and there, and then basically live what they have decided (mostly by tradition or a moral conscience) is a proper Christian life.

My own spiritual growth came in fits and spurts. I loved intensive weekends and focused trainings and camps and such, but consistency in studying on my own was a problem.

In 2008, one year before I started A Slob Comes Clean, I began attending an intensive weekly Bible study. I was scared to do it, but I heard wonderful things about the children's program and I wanted it for my kids.

I was petrified of the intensity. Of the structure. Of the expectations. I had never been good at consistently studying the Bible and I feared I would fail.

But once I got there, I loved it. For the first several months, I fought back tears of joy every time I walked into the building. I learned so much and loved the passion and purposefulness of the women involved.

It was a beautiful thing.

I loved hearing wisdom shared by women in my discussion group. I would think to myself . . . "The *next* time I do this study, I'm going to put more into it. I want to get that much out of it too!"

Which is warped.

Here's the thing. I wasn't doing it right. Instead of doing a little each day as the study instructed, I was waiting until Tuesday night to rush through my lesson and answer the most obvious questions. Kind of like how instead of doing a little every day, I'd rush around frantically cleaning before someone showed up at my door.

But then I learned you don't get to do the same study twice. You only get one chance. It's a unique feature of this particular Bible Study.

I panicked. I wouldn't GET a second chance? The panic made me examine how I was spending my time. *How I was wasting my time.*

I was sure I didn't have a specific time of day I could consistently devote to studying.

But I *did* sit down and sip a cup of coffee every day at the same time.

It was my routine. As soon as I returned from taking my oldest son to school, I turned on the computer and enjoyed my coffee while I surfed the internet looking for coupon deals.

I felt guilty when I realized this, but I resisted changing. I LOVED that time of day. My internal whining focused mostly . . . on the coffee.

Childish, I know.

I finally realized I could drink my coffee while I did my Bible lesson.

It was so obvious, but had been *so **not** obvious* to me before.

Within a week, my Bible study time (when I drank my single daily cup of coffee) became my favorite time of the day.

Through consistency, I began to see the truth about Bible study.

I had been afraid because I always thought of intensive Bible study as an academic pursuit.

I thought studying the Bible was all about me and what I did. That it was about effort.

Instead, *through consistency*, I began to see how alive the Bible is. I know this can sound crazy to the non-Christian, but the Bible truly is (as it claims) the living, breathing Word of God. (Not that hot breath comes off the pages on a cold day.)

When you really read it and think on it and ask God to help you apply it, the Bible will hit you right in the gut. In *your* gut. Not in some hmmm-what-can-I-learn-from-what-happened-to-some-guy-in-ancient-Isreal way, but in a wow-how-in-the-world-did-the-guy-who-wrote-this-know-exactly-what-I-needed-God-to-tell-me-today way.

It's honestly a little freaky. But also incredibly exciting.

During the first year of that Bible Study, God changed me. Bigtime. I'd been a missionary, I lived in faith in Him, but my relationship with God was becoming more personal and alive than it had ever been before.

And a strange thing happened when I rearranged my day to start it with Bible Study instead of computer time. I got more done. My house was a little cleaner than it had been. That slight shift made a slight difference. About a week into my new routine, I had hope that THIS was the magic pill I'd been hoping to find. Maybe this was the Lightbulb Moment that would change me and change my home and solve my messiness issues once and for all!

But it wasn't.

Life happened, and I kept struggling and being baffled by my seeming inability to keep my house under control.

It was better, but it wasn't good enough. Definitely not good enough to let me justify the blog I so desperately wanted to start.

THE DAY GOD SPOKE

It was August of 2009. I was sitting in church, but I wasn't listening to the sermon. Instead of listening, I was crying out to God in my heart.

My life was going to change the next day. My second child would start kindergarten. I would only have ONE child at home during the school day.

My world was shifting into the future. In the years when I held three little hands (two in one hand and one in the other) to walk through the grocery store parking lot, I don't think I believed the day would really come when life would be different.

Three kids aged four and under (then five and under and six and under) is all-consuming. Someone always needs something.

But things were changing.

For the first time in six years, *I wouldn't have to coordinate naptimes.*

This . . . is a big deal. If you're a mom, you know this. As long as more than one napper lives in the house, there's no guarantee of uninterrupted time. I had visions of softly closing my daughter's bedroom door and sneaking off to the computer . . . to blog.

It was the perfect time to start a blog. I was (almost) guaranteed an hour-and-a-half each day, (maybe two whole hours!!) to **write**.

But I couldn't. Because of this *thing*. This messiness issue I'd never been able to conquer.

Honestly, I was angry. I couldn't understand why God hadn't answered my prayers. I had pleaded with Him to remove this ~~messiness~~ **thing** from me. I had asked Him to change me.

I had begged.

Yet it was the thing I couldn't conquer. The thing that boggled my usually-in-control mind.

And I asked God (not terribly reverently) . . . why? *Why* hadn't He removed this thing I hated about myself? Why hadn't He *changed* me?

I didn't understand. My reasons for wanting to change were noble. I wanted to do something I firmly believed had been placed as a burning desire within me by God. I wanted to do something *good*.

I wanted to encourage women. Moms. I wanted to reach out and affirm their desire to follow God in this crazy motherhood journey.

And yet the very thing God wouldn't remove from me was keeping me from serving Him. From using the gifts and passions **HE** gave me!

As I cried out in my heart, I *heard* God say (I don't say that lightly and I don't say it often) . . . "Write about that."

What?

*Write about **that**?*

About my struggles to get my messy house under control?

Hmmmm. That's actually a really good idea, God.

I'd write about getting my house under control. I could use blogging (the thing I was desperate to do) to KEEP my focus on my home. My home wouldn't suffer from blogging, it would benefit.

In, like . . . a month or two, my house would be perfect! Then I could start my REAL blog!

I loved it. My mind started churning with how it would all work.

Right then, the name of my blog came to me. A Slob Comes Clean.

Now, let me clarify here and now that "slob" is a terrible word. It makes me cringe. I did **not** want to use it.

Over the years, I had called myself "organizationally challenged" or "chronically disorganized" but I often said, "but I'm NOT a slob."

I didn't want to use that horrible word.

I tried and tried . . . but could not come up with another word until right after I set up the blog.

At that point, it seemed too late.

I'd set up the blog as fast as I possibly could. I threw my year-and-a-half of "best practices research" out the window and gave in to Google's promise that I could "have a blog up and running in minutes."

I was desperate. Desperate to act on what seemed to be a God-given idea. Desperate to see if what appeared to be a genius, focus-providing strategy could actually work.

Besides, this wasn't my real blog. *What did it matter if I didn't do things exactly the right way?*

This . . . was a **practice** blog. A way to justify blogging. A way to get my home under control while also learning things I could use when I started my "real" blog.

A total win-win.

But I didn't just set up the blog. I created a new email address. I made up a fake name.

I called myself "Nony" which is short for aNONYmous. I used Blanco for a last name since that's Spanish for "White" (my real last name).

I was petrified someone I knew would find my blog. I wanted to be sure this deep, dark secret I was putting on the internet could never (ever ***ever***) be traced back to me.

Ever.

And the next day, the first day my second child was in kindergarten, I wrote my first post. I called it "Here we go."

In it, I promised (my non-existent readers) complete honesty. I pledged to stop making excuses. I was determined to figure out why I was this way and what I could do to change.

Using the word "slob" helped me start down that path of truth. Once I used that terrible, awful word . . . there was nothing worse that could happen. There was no hiding. The minute someone landed on this new blog I'd created, they would know the thing about me that I tried to keep hidden.

They'd know I am a slob.

When I say I didn't tell anyone, I mean it. I didn't tell ANYone. I didn't tell my husband or my mother or my best friend or my children.

I was used to failing every time I tried a new method to get my house under control. Those who were closest to me knew what a struggle this was for me because they were the only ones (in the whole wide world) who had actually seen how bad it could really be.

WHERE DO I START?

I started in the kitchen.

I had tried every method I'd found, and failed at all of them. I decided I was going to stop worrying about methods and just figure out how to keep my kitchen clean.

My kitchen was *always* a source of frustration. ALWAYS.

When I'd get the itch to clean up my house (or when I knew I *had* to clean it up because guests were coming), I always had to start in the kitchen.

Five hours (or more) later, when the kitchen was finally clean, I was too tired to move to the rest of the house, so my house never gained any real traction.

But I had this thought: If my kitchen was already clean, I could use those five hours to work on the rest of the house.

I knew it was possible. I had been in homes (even when the owners weren't expecting guests!) that *didn't* have a kitchen sink and counters piled high with dirty dishes.

I just had no idea how people managed to do that.

I started washing the dishes. I didn't worry about *how* to wash them, *I just washed them.*

I didn't research the very best way to keep them washed consistently. ***I just washed them***.

And then the next day, I washed them again. Which was ever-so-much harder than it was the day before. It was hard for me to see the point of washing dishes that weren't even piled past the top of the sink. I'd heard people talk about not being able to sleep with dishes in the sink (which had NEVER been a problem for me . . .) but even though wasting my time on a little ol' pile of dirties seemed fruitless, I had to acknowledge that those non-sleepers had clean kitchens. They must know something I didn't know.

As I washed dishes day after day, it started to feel normal. Not fun, but normal.

Like, I didn't feel awkward the way I once did, and because I was doing them every single day, there weren't many to do. After a week, I wasn't overwhelmed by dishes anymore and I added another task.

On the blog, I called these my non-negotiable tasks. I took the time I needed to turn the tasks into habits. Generally, seven days worked. They didn't become automatic after a week, just not overwhelming.

With each non-dramatic task, I saw huge improvements in our home.

I didn't make plans. I just lived day by day. In the moment.

I didn't start with a list of daily tasks a mile long. (I had always done that before.)

I just focused on one thing that boggled my mind until it no longer boggled my mind. And my house started to look better. Much better. Just by doing piddly, daily tasks. No top-to-bottom clean to get started, just small tasks done over and over.

MY FIRST COMMENT

As I worked in my home, I wrote on the blog. I shared what I was doing and the crazy thoughts that went through my head. I showed pictures of my messy rooms as I worked to declutter them.

I was petrified to get my first comment. I was convinced it would be from someone too horrified to keep his/her mouth shut. He/she would feel the need to express what anyone else who had accidentally landed on my blog had obviously felt as they read the confessions I posted.

But that didn't happen. In fact, my first comment (and my first 1,000 comments) weren't from people shocked and horrified at all. They were from Kindred Spirits. From people who claimed my humiliating confessions echoed the thoughts that went through their heads. That *my* struggles were *their* struggles too.

When you first start a blog, every new reader makes you jump up from your desk and do a little happy dance. You click on each name and find out everything you can about this person who commented! As I did this, I learned something. I *liked* these women.

They were creative. Intelligent. They were poets and artists and theatre teachers (LOTS of theatre teachers!)

They were like me.

The common thread I saw time and time again was creativity.

I began to see a direct relationship between creativity (the thing I love about me) and my Slob Problem (the thing I despised about me).

And somehow, knowing that made things better.

This is the second reason I'm so glad I used the word "slob." **It helped me accept that being a slob is part of who I am.** It's how my brain works. I'm wired to be creative, and part of that wiring causes me to see the world differently than Normal People see it. I love that about myself, but seeing the world differently also has something to do with why I struggle with housework.

Accepting myself didn't mean I accepted the messiness. Instead, it gave me freedom to stop feeling like a failure when typical organizing advice didn't work for me. Most organizing advice is written by organized people. Their brains don't work like my brain works, and that's okay. I just needed to find ways to keep my home under control that worked for me. For my unique brain.

ME WORKING ON MY HOUSE
GOD WORKING IN ME

The second year of the Super Intensive Bible Study began just a few weeks after I started A Slob Comes Clean. Again, I was amazed at how relevant the study was to what was going on in my life.

That year, we studied the book of John. John is in the New Testament of the Bible and tells about Jesus's life on earth. As we studied (and I was *really* studying now that I had a routine), the word "purpose" kept coming to mind. I saw again and again how each and every moment of Jesus's earthly life had purpose. Every word He spoke, every look He gave, every choice He made had a purpose. People saw what He did, understood the completeness of God's plan better from what they saw, and wrote about it so I can understand too.

And God began speaking to me about my own purpose. About not wasting words or breath or choices. As I saw the far-reaching effects of Jesus living in the moment with purpose, I began to be more willing to embrace where I was in life.

Exactly where I was. In a small town. It's a small town that isn't dramatic or exciting and doesn't produce a look of awe on anyone's face who finds out where we live.

It's pretty boring compared to Bangkok or Africa or wherever I assumed I would live when I was practicing those Bathtub Speeches as a child. But as the word "purpose" weaved its way in and around my year, I finally let go. I let go of my excuses for not doing more if only I had a more exciting place to do it.

I saw that purpose isn't something for me to find. It's something for me to accept. Wherever I am, whatever my circumstances, God has something for me to do right then and there. Waiting to find that purpose is just missing it. The purpose is now.

At the same time I was learning this, the blog was gaining some momentum. Not anything huge, but I was getting comments pretty regularly. People were beginning to share that they were so glad to find someone else who thought the way they did. They were excited to learn they weren't alone.

This totally gave me warm fuzzies.

I know *now* that MANY people struggle the way I did/do, but before I started the blog, I really thought I was the only one.

About four months into blogging, I said to my husband, "Ummm, I think I might actually have something here." I could see there was a need for me to do what I was doing. Both in our home AND for the benefit of those who were commenting and emailing to let me know they were gaining hope watching my journey.

So the spiritual work going on in my heart was like a seed being planted.

The seed was acceptance.

Acceptance that wherever I was in life, that was where I was supposed to be. I was supposed to live in that place with purpose and with the goal to help others understand God's desire to know them too.

I began to accept the need for a Slob Blog in the world, and I was accepting my own circumstances as no accident.

But I wasn't putting it all together just yet.

BLOGGING GETS MORE SERIOUS AND I SHOW MY FACE

The blog grew. Not by leaps and bounds, but it grew. I was figuring out blogging strategies and practicing them. (So I could do my "real" blog correctly when the time came.)

I found out about a new blogging conference. It was run by a group of women I highly respected. I knew their blogs. They were family-focused but also business focused. They took blogging-as-a-job seriously, but put their families first.

When I saw they were putting on an intensive learning event (a conference), I didn't think it made sense to go. I wasn't treating blogging like a business yet because I wouldn't let myself. My youngest child was still at home full time and I didn't want to devote myself fully to blogging until she was in school.

(Tunnel-vision, remember?)

But . . . they were requiring an application process, and there was a five dollar fee to apply.

I don't know why, but that fee made me apply. I was so incredibly confident I *wouldn't* be accepted that I couldn't help myself.

And then I was accepted.

Suddenly, I started to wonder if maybe I did have something worth sharing with the world. There was something so very affirming about being chosen, and my confidence grew.

My husband and I felt I HAD to go (having been *accepted* and all), so we turned it into a family vacation.

I .... was .... petrified.

For the first time ever, I was going to introduce myself to people, in REAL life (flesh-and-blood, face-to-face, look-them-in-the-eye) . . . as a slob.

I was going to tell them my deep, dark secret in the first moment we met.

Yikes.

At this point, only a few people knew: my husband, my mom and dad, and my best friend.

Oh, and my aunt. My father couldn't stand the pressure and let it slip.

Let me take a second and explain something that made no sense to me. When I say my father couldn't stand keeping the secret about my blog, I mean he was bursting with pride.

Which boggled my mind.

I couldn't believe how the people in my life reacted to me telling the world I was a slob.

My husband only had one complaint about my blog. It was not that I showed pictures of our laundry piles and unmade bed. *It was that he couldn't tell anyone about it.*

He was so proud of me.

Bizarre, right? They weren't the least bit ashamed that I was writing about my most embarrassing secret. *They were just thrilled I was writing.* They were happy I was using my gifts and they cheered me on each time I hit a new traffic milestone.

This was mind-boggling to the girl who had always worked so hard to hide her flaws.

But even though my family and closest friends had all been shockingly supportive, the conference would be different. I was going to tell *random strangers* I was a slob. **That was the only way they would know me.**

When I went, though, I only felt acceptance. And for the first time, I had people tell me face-to-face that they related to my struggles.

It was crazy.

But most of all, these lovely women who blogged about lovely things encouraged me to run with it. They blew off my protestations that A Slob Comes Clean was only my practice blog. They brainstormed for me and cheered me on in accepting the potential of a blog about being a slob.

I still wasn't convinced.

At least not completely. But I did begin to make a few very small changes. First of all, I added a picture of myself.

Granted, it was a picture designed to escape the notice of anyone I knew in real life who accidentally landed on my blog . . . but it was a picture. Showing my face invested me a little more in this crazy Slob Blog thing I was doing.

Note: I later found out that almost everyone who applied was accepted to that conference. I'm still amazed, though, at how much of an impact thinking I was "worthy" made on my confidence.

Another note: Those were new-out-of-the-package rubber gloves. I promise.

THE BLOG'S SECOND YEAR

Year Two of the blog was Year Three of doing the ultra-serious-and-involved Bible Study that had changed my spiritual life. It was also my last year with my daughter at home full-time.

The thought never even crossed my mind that I would NOT attend the study.

The first week, I be-bopped into the building, so excited to get started. Summer's innate loosi-goosiness makes it difficult for me to stay focused and consistent studying the Bible. I was craving the structure. I *needed* the structure.

I'm pretty sure I glowed. And breathed multiple sighs of relief when I walked through the door.

The second week, as I left the church, I heard a still, small voice say, "You're not supposed to be here."

I physically shook my head to get that voice out. Obviously, that was NOT God. I knew enough to know that wouldn't make a *lick* of sense. (When I get high-and-mighty, my Texan slang comes out. Sorry.)

I kept on walking and kept on smiling. And pretended the ultra-disconcerting thought/voice hadn't spoken.

But the next week, I heard it again.

If you're not a Christian, I'm pretty sure you think I'm bonkers. Hearing voices? *That's kindof the definition of bonkers, right?*

It wasn't audible, but it was clear. Perhaps a non-Christianese way to say it is: A Moment of Clarity.

A Moment of Extreme Clarity.

Extreme Clarity that didn't come from anywhere inside my own brain. And yet I recognized it. After two years of consistently studying the Bible and experiencing again and again what it's like to let God shape my heart and mind, I recognized it.

Once recognition happened, I could no longer ignore the voice, no matter how much I despised/feared/rejected what it was saying.

So I asked (again, *not out loud . . .*), "What?? That makes NO sense! Why in the world would you NOT want me here? This is a **good** thing. A perfect thing. THE thing I NEED to stay close and hear your voice!!!"

The next week, after having pushed back against that voice for seven whole days, He spoke at the beginning of the Bible study time. As I sat in my small group, I started blubbering.

Oh my word, I can't paint a proper word picture of the scene. I am the complete opposite of a pretty crier. Ugly Cry doesn't describe it.

This was Ugly Cry Extreme. The kind where I gulp and choke and can't stop the snot from pouring out of my nose.

I left the room. I blotted my face with wet paper towels, and went back.

When the last discussion question, "How can the group pray for you?" was asked, I felt I owed an explanation to the group of ladies who didn't really know me yet but were gracing me with nervous, encouraging smiles.

Me: (jagged breath and squeaky voice) I think God is telling me I'm not supposed to be here.

Them: (eyes widening, heads shifting slightly in confusion)

Me: I don't understand. I have no idea *why* He would want me to give up THE thing that has brought me closer to Him. THE thing that has caused me to grow spiritually over the past two years. Y'all know I'm the biggest BSF cheerleader ever. I LOVE this study!

And they prayed for me. Not that God would change His mind (the way I wanted them to pray), but that I would do whatever God was asking me to do.

After discussion time came lecture time. I held my breath to keep from sobbing while tears streamed down my blotchy, swollen face.

I picked up my daughter and ran to the car, desperate to sob again.

I cried for hours, and kept crying for days. The next week, I was still crying.

It was horrible.

Finally, I said, "OK."

I had no idea why, but I knew God was telling me He didn't want me going to BSF right then.

One night that week, in bed, I sputtered out my despair and my decision to not go back if that was what God was asking of me. My poor, sweet husband widened his eyes at my tear-stained, lacking-the-beauty-to-which-he-is-accustomed face. He was confused as well. He'd seen the difference in me. He knew how much I loved this study.

While I cried, I prayed. I asked and questioned and begged God to change His mind. He began to show me why we were having this conversation.

Before the Bible Study had started that year, I was asked to be on a team at our church. The team's purpose was to determine our church's identity and what we needed in a new pastor. A consultant came in, and he assigned extensive Bible reading.

In my heart, I said, "Ummm, I don't *need* to read what you're telling us to read. I . . . do **B.S.F.**"

In case you didn't read that with the 80s Valley Girl intonation in which it was said (inside my head), I was being snotty.

I was being prideful.

And ultimately, I was putting my faith in a Bible Study.

What??

As the week went on, I began to see I had put this particular organization on a pedestal. I was holding on so tightly, by my fingernails, because I truly believed that without this study, I couldn't enjoy the amazing and life-changing relationship I had developed with God over the past two years.

And God said very simply, "It's not the study. It's me."

As a good Christian, I knew this. But obviously, I didn't really believe it.

All week, I prayed. I made the decision to not go back. I was still asking God to change His mind, but I was not planning for His answer to be yes.

The next Wednesday morning, I didn't get dressed. I dropped the boys at school in my pajamas, came home and got down on my knees by my bed while my daughter watched cartoons in the living room.

I was exhausted from my week of resisting, of arguing, of finally accepting.

But I asked one more time. "Please? I get it now. I get that it's You. Not the study. I get that I was depending on the study when you want me to depend on You. But I'm going to ask again, Can I please go back?"

And the still, small voice spoke. "OK. Go today. Next week, ask again."

I threw on a bra as fast as I could and hurried my daughter out the door. We missed the small group discussion time, but I sat in the lecture in total peace.

Week after week, I went back, but it was different. I knew each week of lessons was a gift from God. It was a tool He didn't need to get through to me, but He allowed me to have it.

And my spiritual life changed from "Wow! I go to BSF!! Which has totally solved my inconsistent Bible Study problems!!!!" to "Step by step, day by day, I'm willing to do whatever God asks of me."

All year long, that was what I learned. As a project-minded problem-solver, I thought I had found an answer to my Inconsistency Woes. I was dependent on that answer.

God wanted me to be dependent on Him.

ON THE BLOG

That year, on the blog, things were growing. I was starting to test the waters of monetizing (making money) and finding some things that worked and plenty that didn't.

I was learning. I was learning I would likely never run out of content. I was learning I had a real writing "voice" that seemed to appeal to more people than just my parents. I was learning how to keep my home under control. I'd moved from total bewilderment to understanding the basics that would keep my house out of chaos.

The blog was gaining a little traction, and people were starting to ask "How to" questions.

I *hated* this.

I would push off the questions and advise people to read from the beginning of the blog to see the process I had been through.

But the questions kept coming.

I tried to claim that the blog was all about me. I was just figuring out things for myself. I knew my own journey was inspiring others in their homes, but I couldn't imagine anyone wanting/taking housekeeping advice from me.

And then, in the spring of that year (I think of years in terms of school years, ok?) I wrote a post about how happy I was to be able to walk into my walk-in closet.

I had worked in my closet and *that* was my big accomplishment. Clearing space in the floor. Not the entire floor, but just enough to be able to walk in and get to the clothes.

Right. Celebrating a walk-on-able floor pretty much separates me from any other blogger in the organizing niche.

The response was great. People who read my blog were happy for me and totally understood that floor space in a closet is exciting.

And then I started getting traffic from an online forum somewhere. This had happened before, and I loved to follow the links back to see what people were saying about me.

I followed this one back and saw that someone had started a thread about decluttering inspiration and had linked to my homepage. The closet post just happened to be my top post that day.

I eagerly read the responses. People were *not* impressed.

In fact, they were cruel. They couldn't believe I was calling that organized! (Which I wasn't.) One said it made her feel better about her husband who is a total slob. It went on and on and even though I can't remember exactly, I know it was bad enough that one person did mention people should be careful since "the person who wrote it" might follow the link back and see what they were saying.

Ouch.

Even though I had assumed I would be inundated with hateful blog comments from the beginning, it had never happened. I had experienced acceptance and love and understanding.

Now let me clarify that these people never left rude comments on my site. I'm sure they felt they were having a private conversation. I also understood what they were saying. They thought they were being directed to an organizing site and ended up seeing after pictures that would be their personal worst-nightmare before pictures.

I got that and was pretty mature and rational about it. They hadn't personally attacked me.

But then, it hit me that they had (indirectly) personally attacked the person who had been inspired by the post. That person was putting herself (himself?) out there as someone who related to a slob. And I know she must have felt personally ridiculed by their comments.

Suddenly, my Mama Bear Side came alive. I was given the gift of Extreme Self Confidence by my parents. I suffer from Excessive Honesty and have learned to (mostly) blow off comments of people who don't take the time to understand.

But not everyone has been given those gifts.

Suddenly, my blog had a new purpose. I saw the value in putting myself out there. I saw the need for SOMEone to be honest. I accepted the need for someone to share her own struggles so others would know they weren't alone.

A passion was lit inside me to *use* this blog. To be that person, even though it still made my stomach hurt to publish really-really-far-from-perfect pictures of my home.

This was a turning point for me and for the blog. It gave me boldness. It helped me connect with my readers in an us-against-the-world way. And it helped me accept that, strangely, I could be a leader of a community of slobs.

So in the year when God was teaching me (again and again and over and over) that He wanted me to live day by day and in total dependence on Him, I was also accepting that this Slob Blogging Thing I was doing was a real thing. A real ministry.

Hmmmm.

MY NEXT BIG BLOGGING MINDSET CHANGE

The next summer, I returned to the same blogging conference. I attended one session that changed me.

It was about YouTube. The YouTube part was interesting, but the part that shook me was the speaker's insistence that **you don't have a blog, you have a message.**

YouTube (or podcasts or whatever else) was another way to get that message to more people, since not everyone reads blogs.

This made me think about what my message was and about the people who needed to hear it.

It helped me grasp the fact that I had something of value to share.

I had hope.

At that point, I'd been blogging for two years. Two years of what I called my "deslobification" process. I'd figured out a lot about myself and had made huge strides in our home.

I knew, without a doubt, there were people who needed my hope.

And God kept working on my heart. He started to show me *this* was the blog He intended for me to have all along. This was HIS plan from the very beginning, He just let me go through what I needed to go through so I would accept that His plan was better than my idea.

And it was.

I can't express the peace that comes from being open. From NOT trying to hide the icky parts.

As I processed in my head what it meant to accept this Slob Blog was the ministry I had so desperately wanted, it just so happened I applied and was accepted as a Women of Faith blogger.

If you know what Women of Faith is, you might be impressed. Don't be.

Women of Faith is an organization that brings Christian speakers and singers together for weekend events all over the U.S.

Women of Faith is impressive. Being a "blogger" for them wasn't. It was really just free tickets in exchange for blog posts before and after.

I assumed God was going to show me some spiritual things about clutter or cleanliness that could help me in my quest for a more inviting home.

Instead, God worked on me through the one session that really wasn't my favorite. I wanted to stick to talking about clutter and dirty dishes. He wanted to focus on me. On my heart.

I put off writing the "after" post for as long as I could.

I was scared.

God was dealing with me about authenticity. About letting people into ~~our lives~~ my life. About letting people see my flaws.

Part of the problem was that I already considered myself authentic. I didn't think I went around pretending to be someone I wasn't.

But while I didn't pretend, I also didn't *mention*.

Didn't mention things like the fact that I had a blog. A blog that was doing fairly well and was taking quite a bit of my time.

I went to Women of Faith, excited to see what God was going to show me about His plans for this ministry I had finally accepted for what it was.

But I wasn't excited about what He actually showed me.

He told me it was time to begin tearing down the walls. It was time to stop segmenting my life. To stop being different people in different places and to be authentic . . . everywhere.

Everywhere.

I couldn't call this my ministry while hiding it from the people who knew me in real life.

Ouch.

When I finally posted, I wrote:

"But God wants me to start working on another aspect. I've been completely authentic here on the blog. It has been my safe place. My place where I can say anything, after editing and deleting and using italics in all the right places.

And I've hidden behind the pink bandana.

But I've been convicted that I need to share more of me . . . everywhere. All of me. This part that was such a small part because I kept it hidden has now become a very large part of my life. And, in a strange way, it has become my ministry. So many of you have shared that you needed someone else to be willing to say the things that go through your own head.

If it's going to be my ministry, I need to be all in. Not just hiding behind a computer screen where I can delete any horrified looks that come my way."

I decided to start by answering questions honestly. With my new phase of life, the most common conversation starter was "So what are you doing now that all your kids are in school?"

"Nothing" was a lie. I was working like a madwoman to do all the things I'd purposely **not** done when my daughter was at home during the day. It was the logical time to be honest.

Not that I immediately gushed it all out. Most conversations went like this:

Them: So what are you doing now that all your kids are in school?

Me: Oh, I'm working at home.

Them: What are you doing?

Me: I'm writing.

Them: Really? What are you writing?

Me: On the internet.

Them: Where on the internet?

Me: I have a website.

Them: What's it about?

Me: Housekeeping

Them: What's it called?

Me: (Gulp) A Slob Comes Clean

And that was how the conversations went. I was more than willing to stop at any point when "they" said, "Oh. Okay."

So while I wasn't running out and shaking hands as Nony, I also wasn't lying to anyone. Or outright hiding.

And I began to learn something. Most people are nice. Most people understand. Very few people are truly horrified.

Mostly, I learned the vast majority of people crave honesty. They usually just need to know that the other person will be honest too. They want to know they'll be accepted for who they really are.

STILL SO FAR FROM PERFECT

Authenticity wasn't the only thing God wanted me to learn that year.

The previous May, after going week-by-week through the Old Testament book of Isaiah, after having my pride (and my dependence on a study rather than on God himself) pounded down into (almost) nothing, I was asked to consider serving in leadership for the Bible Study the next year.

I feel the need to explain. Committing to serve as a leader in this particular Bible study means being there two days each week. One day, the leaders have their own prayer, discussion and training time. The next day, they serve as leaders.

I *knew* it was a huge commitment. I also knew I was planning to turn my blog into a business at the same time.

But . . . there was a reason I desperately wanted to do it.

As I mentioned earlier, this particular Bible Study has a rule that you can only do each year-long study once. It's a worldwide organization, and many of its groups have waiting lists. The only people who are guaranteed to be able to repeat studies are . . . leaders.

Right.

I wanted to be in leadership because I wanted to be in this Bible Study for the rest of my entire life.

Yes. I had put it in its place, but still . . .

You can't volunteer for leadership. You have to be asked. I panicked, wondering if this would be my only chance.

Officially, I prayed about it, but the prayer went something like this: "Ummm God? I really want to do leadership in BSF next year and I think I'm going to do it. K? Bye."

Really. *I know better.* I've heard that "still, small voice" enough times to know that making a statement and sticking my fingers in my spiritual ears because I don't want to actually hear an answer . . . isn't praying.

Ugh.

Although God worked in me and through me, it was a miserable year.

Mis-er-a-ble.

Once the school year (and new blog year, and new Bible Study year) got going, I was overwhelmed. Right from the beginning.

I was away from home two days each week for BSF. Almost every week, another random "opportunity" would arise to volunteer at the kids' schools or at church. As I turned the blog into a business, it immediately began demanding more time and attention. I was starting to take on freelance writing assignments. Three (often two) days were simply not enough time to do everything I needed to do.

It was a year of feeling frantic, overwhelmed and defeated. **All** the time.

Looking back, I know the feeling of not being enough, of not having enough time or brain power or energy or *anything* to be able to accomplish what I needed to accomplish was exactly where I needed to be to learn what I needed to learn.

In this year when I was wild-eyed and out-of-breath and on-the-verge-of-tears-at-any-given-moment from the start, we studied the New Testament book of Acts and the letters written by Paul as he went on his missionary journeys.

In the years before, God had shown me that my purpose is in my everyday reality. That I'm not enough, so I need to stop trying to be enough and let Him be my More Than Enough.

He wants the best for me, and the best for me is Him.

But what does that look like? How does that actually work in my everyday life?

The beauty of studying the book of Acts and Paul's letters is that those questions are answered. Christianity was a brand new thing. It wasn't even called Christianity yet. People just knew that Jesus was the way to have a personal relationship with the one true God.

Paul's passion was to teach people what it actually meant to live as a follower of Christ.

In his letters, he explained over and over and in various ways, HOW to live in faith. This was what I needed.

If I can't do this on my own, *then how do I do it?*

First, in the midst of the craziness and life pulling me in every direction imaginable, I had to identify what mattered. In 2nd Corinthians, Paul talks about God's glory. And how that's what it's *all* about. Being a Christian? It's all for God's glory. Living? Working? Speaking? All for God's glory.

See, I'm living as a letter. A letter from Christ. The Apostle Paul said it like this:

"You yourselves are our letter, written on our hearts, known and read by everybody. You show that **you are a letter from Christ**, the result of our ministry, written not with ink but with the Spirit of the living God, not on tablets of stone but on tablets of human hearts."

I'm the letter. People see me? They're seeing God. Actually, they see God when they see *inside* my heart, because *that's where the letter is written*. And the Spirit (who is God) is the ink. He doesn't just write the words people are seeing. He IS the words people are seeing.

That's my purpose. My purpose isn't about me.

It's to let people see God living in me.

"Being a Christian" isn't just my sins being removed so I can go to heaven, it's God's righteousness (holiness/absence-of-sin) being placed on me. Jesus, who is God, gave me Himself, His holiness.

And He is light. Pure light. The source of light. And He "made His light shine in our hearts . . . "

He's in me. The ink of the letter and the light in my heart.

I think I knew all that, but the practicality of what I realized next was life-changing, career-affirming, and mind-boggling.

2nd Corinthians 4:7: "But we have this treasure (talking about that light in our hearts) in jars of clay **to show that this all-surpassing power is from God and not from us**."

And then my Bible Study leader said something like this: "We're jars of clay. We're fragile. But when our jars of clay crack, it's through the cracks that God's glory shines."

I'm a jar of clay. I'm fragile.

But that's okay. The cracks that happen when I'm not strong enough to handle the pressure let people see what's inside.

And what's inside is amazing.

The same Holy Spirit who had the power to raise Jesus from the dead lives in me.

His glory . . . shines through my cracks.

Ton. Of. Bricks.

This was the year when God had been dealing with me very specifically about authenticity. About honesty. About being the same me everywhere. He'd also given me a ministry totally based on the *very* thing I'm NOT good at! The thing I DIDN'T want to share!

He was working to get me to **stop trying to cover up all those cracks**. To show me that **struggles are there to produce the cracks that let people see HIM inside.**

(And oh my word, if keeping the house clean is my biggest struggle, I have it **good**!)

His glory shines through the cracks.

Wow.

My cracks have purpose.

This was big.

It's one thing to know I have purpose. That my life, as is, is exactly where I'm supposed to be fulfilling that purpose. But the bad things (the things I'd prefer to hide) have purpose too? Really? The broken, imperfect parts?

Which leads to the next knock-me-over-and-drag-me-out-of-the-room part.

Weakness.

I'd heard in Sunday School all my life that Paul (the one who wrote all this) had a thorn in his side (not an actual thorn, but something he hated about himself) that God chose not to take away even though Paul asked Him repeatedly to take it away.

I thought it was a story showing that sometimes the answer to a prayer is "no."

On a very basic level, that's true. But there was soooo much more for me to understand.

In 2 Corinthians 12, Paul shares that he could boast about **a lot** of things. God did amazing miracles in his life. He had stories that would keep crowds on the edges of their seats and produce thunderous applause and gasps of awe.

And yet "**To keep me** from becoming conceited because of these surpassingly great revelations, **there was given me a thorn in my flesh**, a messenger of Satan, to torment me. Three times I pleaded with the Lord to take it away from me. But he said to me, 'My grace is sufficient for you, for my power is made perfect in your weakness.' Therefore I will boast all the more gladly about my weaknesses, so that Christ's power may rest on me. That is why, for Christ's sake, **I delight in weaknesses, in insults, in hardships, in persecutions, in difficulties. For when I am weak, then I am strong."**

The Bible never reveals Paul's weakness.

But I understand the feelings he expressed. I might *think* I'd like to show the world how to be a perfect mom and wife, but if I did that . . . my natural tendency toward being prideful would flare up, and I would only set myself up for failure because I'm *not* a perfect mom or wife.

Instead, I get the blessing of sharing my deepest, darkest secret with the world. I get to avoid pride because of the little ache in the pit of my stomach every time I tell someone what it is that I "do."

God gave me my gifts. He wants me to give Him my weakness.

Through my weakness, *the cracks*, people see that any light from within is not from me, it's from God.

And I'm so thankful.

I wanted a blog. I wanted a ministry. I wanted a purpose. I wanted desperately to scratch my never-ending creative itch and I wanted to make an impact.

I wanted to encourage women.

I get to do all of those things in a bigger, more exciting way than I ever thought possible.

He answered every prayer and every desire of my control-freak heart. He just answered them far differently than I ever imagined.

He said, "No, I won't remove your weakness, but I'll use it."

His way is ever-so-much better. I have freedom. I am free to be completely honest. I have nothing to hide.

He has shown me (and continues to show me again and again) that the richness in my relationship with Him happens when I give Him all of me.

Even the very worst of me.

God doesn't care about the clutter. He cares about my heart.

Sure, less stuff helps my family function and lets me serve Him better. A kitchen counter that isn't covered in dishes means I'll open my front door more readily and I can welcome someone in who needs to know they're loved. All that is great and valuable.

But God just wants me. The real me. The come-as-I-am me. A clean kitchen doesn't get me any closer or farther from heaven. He's the only way anyway, and nothing I do or don't do affects our permanent relationship.

He cares about my *heart* and my willingness to let Him use me to show His intense love and his awe-inspiring glory to others.

He never shared my delusions that I would/could be perfect anyway.

I wanted to give my talents, my passions, and my abilities to God.

I wanted to give Him my gifts.

But that doesn't make any sense. Those *gifts* are called *gifts* because they were **given** to me.

By God.

He's the one who gave **me** my gifts.

What He wants from me . . . is my weakness. He wants me to give Him the part of me that I try to hide. He wants me to stop holding onto the thing that I've decided He can't possibly use.

The ugly part.

God wants the worst of me.

FIVE YEARS IN

A Slob Comes Clean has been going for more than five years now.

So what has happened in the two years between the my-cracks-have-purpose revelation and the release of this book?

In that cracks-have-purpose year, 2012, I wrote my first e-book, *28 Days to Hope for Your Home*. Putting a deslobification guide out into the world meant I officially accepted I have something real and valuable to share.

I also started speaking about cleaning and organizing. Though I've always enjoyed public speaking, I never (ever ever) thought I'd speak about *that*. At the end of that year, someone in my church heard a rumor I "speak" and asked me to share at a women's event, even though she had no idea what my topic would be. As hard as it was to talk about my deep, dark secret in front of people who really knew me, it was the perfect way to finish the year in obedience to God's request that I embrace this ministry He had given me.

I stepped down from leadership in BSF the following year, and in the fall of 2013 I stopped going. My mother-in-law's health was declining rapidly and I needed to commit to driving an hour each way to help her out one day a week. Because of that difficult, over-committed year, I knew it wasn't possible to help her AND attend the Bible study. I miss it, but I still love my Bible/coffee/time every morning and have turned to journaling as a way to stay focused.

God has continued to show me, through studying the imperfect and inconsistent people He chose to use, that it's still about the day-by-day. God wants me to give Him each day as it comes. When I fail (as so many "great" people in the Bible did), He wants me to take a deep breath and keep going.

The blog has also grown significantly and I've added video, podcasts and more e-books to the mix. There is a true community of women who seek to better their homes and who gain inspiration from each other and encourage without judging.

I love it.

After I wrote my third e-book, *Drowning in Clutter?* and my "platform" grew even more, I felt a nudging/kick-in-the-rear to write *this* book. It has taken me a very long time to write it and I've put many other Big Ideas on hold so I could get it done.

Here's the thing.

A platform of well-over 100,000 people is great. While I love that people credit me for their clean(er) kitchens, every single thing that's happened through this blog will be absolutely nothing if I don't share the one thing that matters.

That one thing is God, and His desire to have a personal relationship with each of us.

I know not everyone wants to hear about that, and I know a cleaning blog isn't the place to start preaching sermons. But the thing that has amazed (and surprised) me about blogging is the reality of the relationships I've formed. If you're a reader, I care about you. I cheer you on and I cry over your struggles. Even if I don't know your name and wouldn't recognize you in a crowd, I have an actual relationship with you.

I care.

And so many of you have let me know you care. It feels like I have personal conversations with thousands of close friends all at once when I write a blog post.

And if this God stuff is for real (and I know from what He's done in me that it is), **I can't *not* share**. It's not enough for you to know I'm a Christian. I want you to know God wants you too.

If you've read this far, and all the God Stuff seems like a crock to you, we're still friends. I hope we're the kind who can share our hearts, and who tell each other what they need to hear even when they know it'll get ignored.

Your acceptance or rejection of God doesn't affect our relationship. It's between you and Him.

Meanwhile, we'll just keep doing our dishes together.

Every single night. Until the end of time . . .

ABOUT THE AUTHOR

Dana K. White is wife to Bob and mom to Jackson, Reid, and Presley. This book tells almost everything about her, so there's not much more to share!

Find Dana all over the internet (Facebook, Twitter, Pinterest, YouTube, podcasts, etc.) or sign up for her daily or weekly email at http://www.aslobcomesclean.com/connect. Email is the very best way to stay connected! If you are ready to start improving your own home, check out http://www.aslobcomesclean.com/my-e-books/ for Dana's other, more instructional books. Dana is available as a speaker..

Finally, she'd love to hear from you! Email Dana at aslobcomesclean@gmail.com.

Made in the USA
Coppell, TX
03 February 2024